PERSEPHONE'S
AND OTHER

GEOFFREY GRIGSON

*Persephone's Flowers
and other Poems*

SECKER & WARBURG
LONDON

First published in England 1986 by
Martin Secker & Warburg Limited
54 Poland Street, London W1V 3DF

Copyright © the estate of Geoffrey Grigson 1986

British Library Cataloguing in Publication Data

Grigson, Geoffrey
  Persephone's flowers and other poems.
  I. Title
  821'.912   PR6013.R744

  ISBN 0–436–18807–4

Typeset by Inforum Ltd, Portsmouth
Printed in Great Britain by
Redwood Burn Ltd, Trowbridge, Wiltshire

CONTENTS

INTENSIFICATION OF THE NIGHT

A plane hums south, and twinkles
Through the pure slate blue of our night.
A three-quarters moon through close
Trees lies on its back.

Shooting stars intensify
The night.

NATURE

In season we indulge
Our noses
With the scent
Of sweetest roses.
Under the tail
Foxes (they say)
Like violets smell.
Gigantic whales, they say as well,
Possess a violet-perfumed
Liver.
O for such smells which do not stale
Praise we the Eternal
Giver.

COLD JANUARY

Cold January, at the beginning
In the trough of the year.
I have much to fear.

Cold January, there is little singing.
In this first week of the year
Few flowers are here.

Cold January, and a wind stinging
This first daylight of the year,
And grey wind-blown hair.

Grey wind-blown hair,
And ice on the squared bark of the pear.

TROUT IN THE MONTH OF MAY

Fresh stayed the scent
In that wet canvas bag
Of broken fern and slime
From fresh-caught trout,
When on the young grass
They slithered out.

WHITE BIRD IN THE COOMBE

If a ghost did exist
And was fancied to scream
Its scream would resemble
This scream of a bird
Afloat in this coombe,
In this Polperro mist,
Half heard, half seen.

PROFILES

Profiles are often to be seen in leaves,
Of beauties seldom, comforting often, and matronly;
Too often, though, of witches, a sharp leaf-nose growing
Towards a sharp leaf-chin,
A consequence of those fairy-tales with which
Our lives and fears begin.

PERSEPHONE'S FLOWERS

Now it's decline, only with hope again
Awaiting a return of birds, or their sweet
Noise, shifting, scarcely heard through
New leaves of river willows.

It's decline now. Now anaemic
Persephone's special flowers naked
And lucid slip again their pale
Mauve through coarse tufts of valley

Pastures, and I pick a few, setting
Their pale mauve with a late yellow
Of daisies, and now hardly see, lacking
Much hope, how in a magic their yellow

And mauve combine. Only the late crowing
Cock in his hen run below unleaving poplars
Across our slothful river now seems, bright
Bird, now sounds, brassy as ever.

THIN-WHITE RECITES THIN WHITE
POEMS HE HAS
WRITTEN –

But not yet. At this moment the poet
Thin-White listens, or it appears so.
I think he said 'Hush!' just now. I think
He is waiting behind this pillar

To hear himself. His wife listens.
She is waiting to hear Thin-White the Poet,
Her husband, who comes next. She is
Doctor Thin-White, Ph.D. in a theoretical

Subject. Her daughters (two), the Misses
Thin-White, appear to listen. They wear
Broderie anglaise – And, ah, yes, now,
Hush, Thin-White recites, and we all

Listen or it appears so. And the poems
He recites are so pleased with themselves,
They are clapping themselves. Such loyalty,
As if to say We are the poems of Thin-White.

PICTURE – NOT BY KONINCK

How they have exploited the rider alone
In the desert empty valley, in what we called
The New World, with no doubt, far off
As he maybe, a gun in his holster.

Devilment will follow. Murder. Making
Love off-screen. Then disappearing, tether
Untied from the bar, into dusty futurity.
There may be an ambush to come, and justice

Or vengeance. After all, living does accord
With this so exploited image, minus,
As a rule, the heroics, rapid reactions,
Triumphs of sharp shooting, satisfaction

Exacted, corpses riddled and huddled. Dark,
Dark is this auditorium, and it smells
Of sweat, and the girl with a torch, before this
Image of living resumes, brings around ices.

A NAVY OF CRUISERS ON A
BLACK POOL

A navy of cruisers on a black
Pool, floating. Arched darkly overhead
A leaf-navy floating, red, brown.
Anonymously a leaf-navy floating.
No current is sufficient to flow down.

Other peculiarities I list here.
Wide-horned cattle, for instance, though
Emparked, they say are wild.
Gardens on crags, foundations
Of royal Saxon palaces.
Cup-and-ring carvings on grey stone.
Rhododendrons where no
Rhododendrons ought to be.
A holy island at high tide.
A ford, a picturesque look-out
To sea, a monkey-puzzle wood,
Two castles, limekilns of gold,
A kipper factory, Norwegian accents
I cannot understand, Grace Darling,
Etcetera, and etcetera.

And yet –

A navy of cruisers on a black
Pool, floating, arched darkly overhead
A leaf-navy floating, red and brown.
Anonymously a leaf-navy floating.
No current sufficient to flow down.

This
I like best.

CHURCHYARDS AND MANOR HOUSES

OK, we die, self-praisers say.
But then
Those shits and shockers
Die as well, those reputation-
Snatchers fail.

Across brick walls
Of suavest manor gardens,
Over these croquet lawns
And graves,
Sounds the solemn bell.

CEMETERY ISLAND

Yet on this lagoon floats a flat island
Crowded with bones, dry scraps, knitted
Closely by ivy, of most ordinary
Death.

A warbler from Libya, migrating, sharp,
Perches en route for life on the
End of a sun-brittle rib of some
Merchant perhaps.

We approach in our long-legged slow hydrofoil
Which has skimmed along gently, breaking curves
Of a shining seepage of oils of
The rainbow,

And we pause, and from land, over rivers,
And vineyards, and roses, feel a breath which has risen
On mountains, which gratefully does not
Speak of death.

ART

What is it but setting masks
On the familiar to separate it
Clearly from familiarity,
And so reveal its strange
Peculiarity?

FORTY FOOT LANE

Does that dry broken fence exist,
In June, to-day, warped lathes held
By copper nails, behind which on tartan
Rugs, in June, we lay, under fresh

Foliage of lime, over dry soft
Leaves of our earlier time? On that long
Afternoon how could I recognise
The present or the future of that time?

US, THEY, THEM

Can that be what they think
About this poet, who made us all
So dizzy?

Can they believe the car he drove
So furiously was only a second-hand
Tin Lizzie?

Are they so incapable of telling
Their preferred flat booze from
The fizzy?

Must exegesis of such balls
In journals keep them all
So busy?

Tout ça change. And serve them right.
How could such pitter-patter put them
In a tizzy?

BITTER COMMENT

A thousand forms of living,
Tonight's TV instructs me,
Wriggle in close weed-thickets
Of that sea.

Give them another hundred
Million, million years,
And I say luckily they will not
Have developed into Man.

CLOCKWORK

He is not tall, he's broad, thick,
His backside's hard, not padded;
Tucked in, small; his feet large,
You might suppose he is deliberately
Pedantic, given to files and knowing
To a minim where is what.
He can't be married, he's never had
Another, girl, child, dog, cat,
In his arms: a cat has carried him.
He likes home, and not abroad;
You say a metal key turns in his back.
  Now: wind him up. Watch him
Waddle. Smack! He's
Hit a table leg, he's tumbled over.
Listen. How he whirrs! Just lift
Him up, and set him on his feet again.

HOME AGAIN

Hectares of alienation left and right
Of the urbanite, en route for the sea,
And on his way back, on a brilliant
Day, now sulphur-backed sunflowers

Droop in decay. There's a noise of cicadas
At night on the way. Who's to say
What shape are they? Then through
The rain. On again, on again.

A nation streaks south to north
Up its great motor-way.
No more thought of the poisonous
Spines sticking up from the sandy
Curves of the bay. Not a glance
At the acres and acres of alien land.

Demands are heaped inside on the mat.
Fetch the cat, and that's that.

HORIZONTALS ARE PEACEFUL

Horizontals are peaceful,   gentle.
   Savage
   Are verticals
Lay down your arms.

Look at this full floating sense
Of moon
In this for ever
Extending olive sky.

Lay down your arms.

A scent floats on conifers
On warm air,
Now it spreads across damp
Smoothed sands,
On the move
Slightly.

     Extend your hands.
     Lay down your arms.

Horizontals are peaceful:

     Lay down your arms:
     Lay down your arms.
     Let there be no alarms.

Horizontals are peaceful,   gentle.
   Savage
   Are verticals,
    'Lay down your arms'

Look at this full floating sense
Of moon
In this for ever
Extending olive sky.

     Lay down your arms.

TODAY'S PAPER

Somewhere someone has been found guilty.
Somewhere someone has been shot,
    Imprisoned, tortured.
Somewhere someone has found release –
Somewhere, but it must be dark,
    Hollow, underground,
In an old-fashioned hole
Which will collapse, there is
    For someone peace.

ANOTHER AUGUST

Calmness is floating now this whole of a moon
Over our rich earth's wide extra ebony,

Below a bar which maybe will shift
Soon a very little, and uncover a planetary star.

And you have seen this all of a great moon
Silvering a long alley across as black

An ebony sea. And consolation is for what may come?
A floating calm? So now, for calm and being consoled,

How long? How long?

CRUMPLEHORN

Wonders met us on our way
To Christmas parties down that hill,
Water crossed below our road, emerged,
And by illusion flowed uphill
To turn Job's water-wheel;
Bamboos came next, and then
That wickedest of men
Out of glistening ivy lunged,
Coloured, turbaned, threatening,
Frightening, vengeful, bold,
That anchored Indian figurehead
Painted chocolate, pink and gold.

FRAGMENT OF HER TEMPLE

Small birds on migration twitter and flit to and fro.
For a second they perch on a pale marble drum
Half hidden in vegetation, of her temple no more
Remaining which warned merchantmen from the fangs
Of wild rocks below, and the name and the fate of one
Drowned merchant we know, a brief poem
Preserving his story although he was wrecked
Here most of two thousand years ago,
Time without pity not having conquered quite, where
These small birds on migration
Round this pale marble drum half hidden
In deep vegetation, indifferently flit.

Cyprus

MAY THE FIFTH

Our earth exhales.

Lilacs are scenting this dark wind.

No sound
But these lilacs'
Intimation
Until suddenly

Thunder, and several morning
Nightingales.

SO MANY GREATEST ONES

So many greatest ones, I read, 'have won
Their case how slowly only on appeal',
And it is true.

Indifferently we saw them vanish
Over black reefs across oblivion's banks of
Slimy swaying
Weed. Yet some felt with delight how after all
A few from their black barge would step,
Below blue once more

To an unlapped firm shore of clear
White sand, where sand-lilies blow and
Sacred guardians

Of the imagined soul appear – a few at least
Who weren't gazetted in an Honours list
And – how shamefully – were vouchsafed no obit
In *The Times*

ENTERING MY EIGHTIETH YEAR

Entering today my eightieth year, after a late breakfast
I settle to presents, and now to writing a poem. It is a day
Recapitulating my years. So far we have had sleet, snow,
Coldest wind from far north, draughts sneaking
Through cracks and positively shaking cut flowers
In their vases, and sunshine, and glittering leaves.

    I have in the past seen flesh which was pink and warm
Turn green and cold, and this morning tears have rolled from me
So that I could not see. To-day the colour I think of is blue.
Not only because blue bays of sky are occurring
Between black shores of cloud. Various things come
Into thought, and these include blue doves
Of columbine hanging in damp grass, and scent
Of primroses and pale yolk and fluff of scented mimosa
                                  around and above
Fallen columns, and Thomas Nashe, son of a neighbouring
                                          parson
Whom my ancestors undoubtedly knew, settling in his day
To writing – how, when and where, and why
In particular, that dust has closed Helen's eye
And Queens have died young and fair. Oddly
In London's *Evening Standard* yesterday a barbarous female
Wrote about Thomas Nashe (friend of Shakespeare)
And she talked only of violence and brothels and forgot
To mention that poem.

    May be what I am thinking of to-day
Strictly is selfish; but on a birthday I am entitled
To think of myself and be thankful; and await a call from
My daughter. After all how could I help being born, and having
Been born, should I not think the best of life so conferred,
In recollection? Even for others.

    There are stuffy short poets whose pretentious
Writings in the human cause fill me with dismay.
To-day let me forget them, and exclude them. Moments ago
Life seemed a driving hell of small flakes of pitiless
Snow. Each car that passes is white-roofed, now changes
Are so sudden, under a cold Pacific; and so far, so far
I have survived; and though I may not see them again,
It won't be long now before primrose-scents of mimosa

At Salamis and curdled primroses along hedges
Of Cornwall recur, and bells peal at Easter for
Marriages, though muffled they peal also for dying,
And, for Time, the Maxingona booms over Venice.
O benedicite, omnia opera. O blue doves
Sipping in that wet bowl of grasses in the sudden
Glittering corner. O if for a life, if for a moment, still
Benedicite, omnia opera.

THE DAUGHTER'S HOUSE

Thinking of that Strange Madness
We are both with, which grows and flares,
Teaches us what seems to be, and dies,
Reminds me of that never finished house

Across the Green; of deal beams,
Bare; lathes naked, steps which do not
Form a stair. A house in sequence
With the inhabited finished pair –

Of red glass, cut into shapes
On a wheel, already in place there.
No floor up or down that non-stair;
Hard curls of plaster. A child

Died. That was why this middle
House never was finished; the old builder's
Sorrow flitted about there, in that skeleton, that
Hollow, of building year after year.

ON A LITERARY EVENING

Does the cap fit? You think we think
It does; and that's your fear.
You whiskey-sodden little
Silly-billy with long hair.

SNOW IMAGE

This snow image does not show how old
He is or how many acts and incidents
He'd forget.

It's true his memory's failing, but
His lips aren't grey and dry, and just as well.
As yet

Not all of us are turned by age
To maudlin orgies
Of regret.

UNFAIR

Why should they earn so little
Because they have no brains,
So much because they're both born with brains?
They're human both, they need
The same to eat, and when they crap, their crap
Slips down the selfsame drains.

GARDEN WARBLER'S NEST

Hung in that trailing ivy
It is so light and slight a nest
Which that smallest bird slips off,
Dipping away. A wearing of hair-roots
So few that this grey light
Shines through, allowing just
A sight of so brown
A weak huddle of soft
Skulls. These are not,
Let us say, skulls of small
Maos or Lenins – no – who may
Grow to shift our slight space-hung
Pivoted world, who as well,
Life being if obstinate,
So frail, required maternal
Shelter in their cold May
From driving hail.

THE GARDENERS

Is there life that needs no spray
Against disease still waiting for us
On corals in most lonely groups
Where turtles dragged bright

Shells at dawning over whitest
Sand to purest seas? What have we yet
To realize? What novelties
Lie yet unknown for us,

Roots holding them? For us
Is all known, all dulled, for us
Nothing at all growing fresh
And cool? Once we tooth –

Necklaced mariners drove
Our quick catamarans up
Shelving sands, and dug, and fenced
Our plots against vengeance

Of hurricanes. Is all new to us then
Now shrivelled and dry, leaving nothing
At all to profit by across that
Once uncontaminated strand?

From worn runways huge jets fly
Off to Colour Photo Land. Fear holds
Me, native to our not after all
So inexhaustible minds.

STEPS IN THIS ROCK

Why in this wild slate
Were these worn steps cut,
And by whom,
And when?
Pallid wood-sage
And brown oak leaves
Are spread over them.

THE AMERICAN GIRL

With a wonder of grace she bends a sweet
Macintoshed body back into their car,
This American girl Miss Cassat has painted,
This girl, with a long narrow face, in her twenties.

For two days we have watched her, at times
In a jumper pale pink as the langoustine
She was tackling, and have loved her young
Gestures, and now by the lough when they're

Leaving, she's taken her snap of this white
Hotel of their last night's love
Making. What does it matter, as they drive
Away, that rain falls, that into a landscape

Painted by Strindberg, they drive
Into black clouds, that out on this lough
White horses are whipped up by squalls?
Feeling it all, we can say she is having her day.

Lough Fyne

DOCKS ON SUNDAY

Offices are shut, great gates to quays are locked.
Clouds are low. Tide lifts, laps, sinks. Dockers sleep late,
Wake, drink. And it rains, too wet to exercise their dogs.
How would it be if sunshine
Suddenly broke out with glorious laughter,
Life forgetting what went before only a minute after?

LILY AMONG THORNS

He watched her die,
His Lily among Thorns,
Then whispered,
Death our mother
Also
Takes me in her arms.

COMPLINE

These holy halma men file in
And bow. Each turns into his stall,
Young, in mid life, old, weak, lame,
Helped by a rubber-footed stick.

So they escape this way, hoping
To teach the rest of us to be
Content, and pray convinced there is
No other or no better way.

One evolution holds us, all the same.
Their need as well is hopeful of
Impossibility, these brown
Robed holy halma men; it holds

Their abbot too, with whom (slowly
They file off again) these holy
Halma men for ever sing, and play
Their useless medieval game.

RESURRECTION

Sometimes a bitter agony, after a hundred
Years or more, stalks from the dark,
And balefully and resentfully looks round.

It exacts a tear or two, but is weak.
It snarls, but there is no blood for it
And, mercifully, it goes again to ground.

Saham Toney

THE SCARLET ROSE

I slept; and then
O how that sweet scarlet
Rose came
Back again.

REMEMBRANCE

O for my two very dear
Dead ones who live,
It is for you that I care,
Not for these stumbling self-conned
Survivors who now
Creep past here
Along this smooth highway
Once in the year.

Armistice Day

ON THE SUNNY DAY OF A WINTER FUNERAL

A ghostly waiter carries cocktails on his tray
Among invited guests crowding my front room to-day.
But yet the list of those invited is not long,
And for whatever reason several would not come.
Did I command sufficient blood to pour into the ground
For them? And some – the waiter fills their glasses
Up and up – are here without a card from me
Whose presence I most bitterly condemn.

CLOUDS TURN GREY

Warning.
While you may, delight in the sweet bright rounded glow
Of the moonstone clouds
This morning,
For nearer night light seems to shine
The opposite way
And these same sweet bright rounded clouds turn
Grey as grey.

LOOKING AT AN OLD PHOTO

So much is granted, so we have that phrase
Taking it for granted, so we take it:
Which too much means not noticing
Until we've lost it.

What sweet shapes are granted,
What lazy sleepings, and entwinings
And awakings, and what strokings. I look
At an old photo: you, bright in loose

Cotton. I look again at stripings which
I had forgotten. That firm placing.
Those wide curtains dividing, and then raising
And in the dark that secret sweet hand-taking.

Along low cliffs, along deserted sands
That barefooted pacing. Those wet ferns
Weeping, and side by side those steps implanted.
What most sweet mutualities we took for granted.

And this air is cold,
And if not so already, soon
We shall be old.

NEAR EASTERN TRAVEL NOTE

How much in our bettered lives we spoil:
Here where a breeze of that soft kind
Poetically we've called a zephyr, blew her
Ashore, below these wild cliffs of gentle pink,
Here where she stepped naked from her shell, through
Murmuring curds of foam, and flat sweet-scented roses
Floated round her in the air, we scrape and scrape
From our rough toes, before we move off
In the car, so very sticky a viciousness of oil.

THE DIPPER

Staring down from that broken, one-arched bridge,
In that vale of water-mint, saint, lead-mine and midge,
I was amazed by that fat black-and-white water bird
Hunting under the current, not at all disturbed.

How could I tell that what I saw then and there
Would live for me still in my eightieth year?

BRIEF INTERRUPTION

It will be Christmas soon
And a featureless full moon
Fades in a pale morning sky.
In supermarkets potted carols
Are going to blare all day,
Odd consequence of what they say
Happened – was it in Bethlehem? –
So long ago, so very far away.

A bomb explodes outside that crowded store.
A death or two, some policemen lose a limb.
Soon enough, blood's washed away. Again
The cash tills go ting ting,
It's profit as before, and all the while
The potted herald angels sing.

IF-ONLY

Ah now If-Only walks in through the door
And with a wry smile of self-depreciation he takes the floor.
And If-Only explains with his jolly flair
How good life would be if only there were . . .

YOU COMBINE-HARVESTERS

You Combine-Harvesters, eager for gain,
On comfortable seats in your machines,
Which rumble all the day (and half the night)
Over this illimitable, sad, poppyless plain,
No old deceits of ancient poetry
Can you retain, in these late years, pale
Combine-Harvesters, avid for grain.

SEA-MILL

Prêtez-moi, seulement, vallons de mon enfance,
Un asile d'un jour pour attendre la mort.

My wild valley opened between hills
With a curved sea-water pond, which mills
Emptied, and clean tides filled.

Broad low wheels, half hidden, slowly
Turned. It was as if what man and nature grew
Now man and nature milled.

This sea-pond emptied. Small delicate
Wading birds flew in and fed there on rich mud
While that sea-pond refilled.

Tides turned, returned, tides topped
The holding wall. These small birds lifted then,
And flew inland and shrilled

Scum now floats on tides that pushed
Boat-loads to cream teas in the hills. Then parents
Sang. Echoes were doubled, children thrilled.

And my sea-pond's filled, but filled
With hard core asphalted for a thousand cars. Now
It's as if some senses are for ever chilled, as if no
Half-natural sweet life can be willed.

West Looe

A VISIT

His two monstrous steel and concrete studios
On this enflamed hillside are boarded up
And barred. Blue wheels of chicory
Circle in long lorry tracks,
And I reflect, now that they've flown him home,
How even absurdly far his art was
From the white arts of Greece and Rome.

They say he drank. His figs ripen with only
Birds to take them, at these concrete corners.
Inside, so I suppose, lie, helter-
Skelter, oily bags of screws and bolts,
Spanners, torn copies of the *New York Review
Of Books*. I thought him an Hephaistos,
Truculent, if not false, and lame –
Glad that round a remnant of his thought
His figs are purpling all the same.

Saché

MAKING POEMS

To write poems
Which are engaging to me
(Putting words, i.e., again into my
    Meaningful order),
How much must I poise my
Senses in equilibrium once more?

To make poems,
Or a single poem, must trivialities
Again seem of genuine
Consequence, when I doubt if they are
    Consequential at all

(So that, for example,
I noticed with genuine concern
This decidedly unpromising soapy,
Grey, universal dishcloth
    Of cloud)?

How much to me
Must I even seem momentarily
Alive – to achieve, not poems,
But even a single poem again? May be
    The next five minutes

May give an answer. At least
On this pad lines are momently
Growing more black, more
Distinct, and more
    Apparently meaningful.

I do regard this
As a good sign, not having felt
For days and days, yes,
For weeks and weeks, anything like
    Writing a poem or a line.

THE CREMATORIUM

A grand advantage – and, if so,
To whom – to pile on a most high
Summit flaming logs, so visible from
Far off surrounding hills, also
From far out to sea, oak logs crackling
And what had been yourself, once,
Vanishing? Well, it argued you
Had known yourself powerful, certainly,
Important, rich; that others politically
Thought so too? Grand flames rose in the dusk,
Then fell, and in solemnity died down.

      Now, friend, if you, or they, can pay – it's not
A grandeur of the dead you join.
That's sure. Dark limousines discreetly sneak
Into the somewhat secret Crematorium
Wood, off a side road outside our town.
Only oak leaves of autumn now fall down
In Crematorium Lane. Widows wear black,
Are secretly ashamed, and almost glad
You've gone. They disappear. Tired attendants
Turn their gas jets down; and yet between *B.
C.* and *Now* I guess that things are much the same.

LABEL

When I'm labelled grizzly bear
Or disgruntled prickly pear,
I do not care.

It is the indignant
Nature of the pack,
One and all, to answer back.

THE WEATHER'S FINE

I do not find that I'm inclined
To suffer from a sense of sin
Or wear my jacket outside in.
As Mr Fish foretells, the weather's fine
In Buxton, Bath and Tunbridge Wells.

WASTE PAPER BASKETS

Nagged at by advertisers' shiny lies
We need waste paper baskets of stupendous size;
Emptied at breakfast time each day, deny who can
These wicker hold-alls save the soul of man.

PICKED UP IN THE BOOKSHOP

It was a gift given,
Faint pencilling on this flyleaf says,
For a birthday in nineteen-o-four,
A most sweet gift, and the giver,
    And the given, are
        Alive no more.

IN THE AISLE

O sad disaster! Say who can but mourn
To see so fair a flower closed in her urn.
Sunday by Sunday I read that trite verse,
Since when by writers well reputed
I have read worse.

Pelynt

NEGLECTED GARDEN

This is the neglected garden's nature, where
    This stinking hogweed forest follows
    The wild garlic of the spring.
    Looking to the west I see quartzite
    Mountains of the Moon framed by cinnamon-
    flaked fuchsia stems which tower thick and very
    Tall along this slate-grey terrace
    Wall, and how grand it is to hear again,
    After all this belting rain, the brown
    Thunder of the waterfall.
        Dahlias through warm weedy soil
    Push up uncalled for year by year,
    And peonies scatter petals on
    The plantain drive; on which as well
    Araucaria nuts shower down.
    Lengthening gaps too interrupt the long
    Slug-nibbled Dwarf Box edging line.

    But round this garden of neglect for me
    How splendidly these laurels shine.

IN THE ELECTRIC CHAIR

For letting mankind do to man
The things they do, God
Should be at Nuremberg, they say.
The judges look severe,
But cannot find a man
Willing to pull the switch
Although their verdict's clear.

MEADOWS AND ASPHODELS

I read in a book of symbols that
The meadow, nourished by the waters of a river,
Is itself a symbol – I do not agree – of sadness
And that asphodels grow only in the true

Meadow of the soul. That may be so:
In the meadow there is no melody of
Trees and leaves, only the silent, uniform
Waves of grass. I know asphodels

Only on a rocky, well drained, warm
Mountain slope, on which for me sadness
Of the soul does not occur.

ACROSS A GULF OF TASTES AND YEARS

Sixty my father was when I was born who
Now am eighty: I was his last shot
For a daughter to replace his much loved
Favourite sister, who died young,
After bearing someone or other whose
Identity or name he did not know, an illegitimate child.
He loved that child as well.

Little there was we did together
Across the gulf of tastes and years.
Little we played together, no cricket,
No croquet and no cards. That he was good
I was aware; but no, we did not read
Together. Yet by accident at least
I knew George Herbert (like himself
A priest) to be the poet he loved best.
His accidental gift that came in time
To me, was his Collected Herbert
Bound and embossed in mid-Victorian
Ebony.

So I too relish versing;
Even now, think flowers and life
Are to be loved. So I too trust
That this, or who knows
Next year's Death may be a not uncomfortable chair.

ALONG THE ENGLISH BORDER

'As birds do drink and strait lift up their heads,
So' – if we reach Heaven – 'must we do the same
The very moment we are dead.'

These delicate clouds I watch swimming from the Severn hills
And distant Wales, and make out, half-hidden
By dry moss, these words across the base
Of his grand, sky-caressed monument,
Believing not one word of his belief.

Yet gentle is my disbelief.

Why should it not be so? Did he not
Love men, and love a Being he fancied
Was their protective Deity as well?

Stinchcombe and the Tyndale
Monument, North Nibley

EARLY START FROM A NORMANDY HOTEL

Standing at this window on a high hotel passage,
I look over an immense smoothness of empty gravel,
Long as the granite façade, watching her in a
Blue dress carrying a small suitcase towards her car.
No one else is there. A single cloud slightly
Shifts across the blue. Leaves seem entirely still,
Though I imagine that a closeness of autumn
Does shake some of them, just a
Little, and that more of that single
Cloud is now visible. Flags
On high masts, a lax row of them,
Announce and celebrate this foreign hotel,
Ready for an autumn fly past.

        Could this granite courtyard etcetera
Be fixed perfectly in these few words, could
These leaf colours be perfectly fixed
With sufficient vivid subtlety in paint, could not our
Consciousness be justified for a while?

        But no. She has reached her car and
Bends with the key. Her little dog nips in,
And settles behind her. She depresses the
Self-starter and shoots somewhat noisily across
The gravel, and soon is invisible among the
Beech trees. She is gone.

        Both of us have
Long foreign journeys ahead of us in this existence.

Audrien, July 11th, 1985

THE LAST POEM

Young, full, white, strong – I watch
Her instrumental arm
Move up, move down,
A cunning old wizened wrist its comrade:
And there is this world
We do not value, this world we soil,
This world we may destroy forever, leaving a recollection
Only of its so ordered harmonies.

The far off hills are gentle
Blue and wide; and darken above
The intervening sea. Ann near me.
So young, full, white, so strong –
I watch her bare instrumental arm move
Up, move down, its comrade a cunning old
Wizened wrist.

At a concert in a Wiltshire farmhouse, early September, 1985

Patricia Calnan, the young violinist, playing in a crowded living room. Geoffrey in an arm chair. His nurse Ann sitting close beside him. A double image of the two young women, Patricia with her harmonies, Ann who had promised him that his death — which he knew to be near — would be easy, not the anguish of destruction he anticipated.